# 50 Canadian Agriculture Recipes

By: Kelly Johnson

# Table of Contents

- Maple-Glazed Roast Chicken
- Wild Rice and Mushroom Pilaf
- Saskatoon Berry Pie
- Bison and Barley Stew
- Butter Tart Squares
- Grilled Arctic Char with Dill Butter
- Poutine with Farm-Fresh Cheese Curds
- Roasted Root Vegetable Medley
- Canadian Lentil Soup
- Honey-Glazed Carrots and Parsnips
- Tourtière (French Canadian Meat Pie)
- Maple Baked Beans
- Apple and Cheddar Salad
- Wheat Berry and Cranberry Salad
- Elk and Mushroom Burgers
- Chokecherry Syrup Pancakes
- Roasted Beets with Goat Cheese
- Smoked Trout with Horseradish Cream
- Barley and Vegetable Stuffed Peppers
- Split Pea and Ham Soup
- Sweet Corn Fritters
- Maple-Glazed Salmon
- Rye Bread with Flax Seeds
- Grilled Asparagus with Lemon Butter
- Baked Oatmeal with Blueberries
- Wild Blueberry Scones
- Beef and Barley Hotpot
- Roasted Pumpkin Soup
- Cranberry-Maple Turkey Meatballs
- Homemade Saskatoon Berry Jam
- Creamy Potato and Leek Soup
- Barley Risotto with Mushrooms
- Maple-Dijon Glazed Pork Chops
- Oatmeal Maple Cookies
- Sunflower Seed Granola

- Canadian Cheddar Biscuits
- Honey-Garlic Glazed Chicken Thighs
- Roasted Garlic and Butternut Squash Soup
- Bison Meatloaf with Wild Rice
- Carrot and Apple Slaw
- Roasted Brussels Sprouts with Maple Bacon
- Barbecue Bison Ribs
- Farmer's Market Vegetable Stir-Fry
- Creamy Corn Chowder
- Rhubarb Crisp with Oat Topping
- Maple Butter Tarts
- Venison Sausage with Roasted Apples
- Spelt Flour Pancakes with Berries
- Roasted Chestnut and Mushroom Soup
- Pumpkin Seed and Cranberry Energy Bites

**Maple-Glazed Roast Chicken**

**Ingredients:**

- 1 whole chicken (about 4-5 lbs)
- 1/4 cup pure maple syrup
- 2 tbsp Dijon mustard
- 2 tbsp unsalted butter, melted
- 2 cloves garlic, minced
- 1 tsp dried thyme
- 1 tsp salt
- 1/2 tsp black pepper
- 1 tbsp apple cider vinegar
- 1 tbsp soy sauce
- 1 tbsp olive oil

**Instructions:**

1. Preheat the oven to 375°F (190°C).
2. In a bowl, whisk together the maple syrup, Dijon mustard, melted butter, garlic, thyme, salt, pepper, apple cider vinegar, soy sauce, and olive oil.
3. Pat the chicken dry with paper towels and place it in a roasting pan.
4. Brush the maple glaze all over the chicken, coating it evenly.
5. Roast in the oven for about 1 hour 15 minutes, basting with the glaze every 20 minutes.
6. Check for doneness by ensuring the internal temperature reaches 165°F (75°C) in the thickest part of the thigh.
7. Remove from the oven and let it rest for 10 minutes before carving.
8. Serve warm with your choice of sides.

## Wild Rice and Mushroom Pilaf

**Ingredients:**

- 1 cup wild rice, rinsed
- 2 cups vegetable or chicken broth
- 1 tbsp butter or olive oil
- 1 small onion, diced
- 2 cloves garlic, minced
- 1 cup mushrooms, sliced
- 1/2 tsp dried thyme
- Salt and pepper to taste
- 1/4 cup chopped parsley

**Instructions:**

1. In a saucepan, bring the broth to a boil. Add wild rice, cover, and simmer for 40-45 minutes until tender.
2. In a skillet, heat butter over medium heat. Sauté onion until soft.
3. Add garlic, mushrooms, thyme, salt, and pepper. Cook until mushrooms are tender.
4. Stir in the cooked wild rice and parsley. Serve warm.

**Saskatoon Berry Pie**

**Ingredients:**

- 2 1/2 cups Saskatoon berries
- 3/4 cup sugar
- 1 tbsp lemon juice
- 1/4 cup water
- 2 tbsp cornstarch
- 1/2 tsp cinnamon
- 1 prepared pie crust

**Instructions:**

1. Preheat oven to 375°F (190°C).
2. In a saucepan, combine berries, sugar, lemon juice, and water. Simmer for 5 minutes.
3. Stir in cornstarch and cinnamon. Cook until thickened.
4. Pour filling into pie crust. Cover with top crust or lattice.
5. Bake for 40-45 minutes until golden brown. Cool before serving.

## Bison and Barley Stew

**Ingredients:**

- 1 lb bison stew meat, cubed
- 1 tbsp oil
- 1 small onion, chopped
- 2 carrots, diced
- 2 celery stalks, diced
- 3 cloves garlic, minced
- 1/2 cup pearl barley
- 4 cups beef or vegetable broth
- 1 tsp dried thyme
- 1 bay leaf
- Salt and pepper to taste

**Instructions:**

1. Heat oil in a pot over medium heat. Brown bison meat.
2. Add onion, carrots, celery, and garlic. Sauté until softened.
3. Stir in barley, broth, thyme, bay leaf, salt, and pepper.
4. Bring to a boil, then reduce heat and simmer for 1.5 hours until tender.
5. Remove bay leaf and serve warm.

# Butter Tart Squares

**Ingredients:**

**Crust:**

- 1 cup all-purpose flour
- 1/4 cup sugar
- 1/2 cup butter, softened

**Filling:**

- 1 cup brown sugar
- 2 eggs
- 1/4 cup butter, melted
- 1 tbsp vinegar
- 1 tsp vanilla extract
- 1/2 cup raisins or chopped pecans

**Instructions:**

1. Preheat oven to 350°F (175°C).
2. Mix crust ingredients and press into a greased baking pan. Bake for 12 minutes.
3. In a bowl, whisk filling ingredients. Pour over crust.
4. Bake for 25 minutes until set. Cool before slicing.

## Grilled Arctic Char with Dill Butter

**Ingredients:**

- 2 Arctic char fillets
- 2 tbsp butter, melted
- 1 tbsp fresh dill, chopped
- 1 tsp lemon zest
- Salt and pepper to taste
- Lemon wedges for serving

**Instructions:**

1. Preheat grill to medium heat.
2. Mix butter, dill, lemon zest, salt, and pepper.
3. Brush fillets with mixture and grill for 4-5 minutes per side.
4. Serve with lemon wedges.

**Poutine with Farm-Fresh Cheese Curds**

**Ingredients:**

- 4 large russet potatoes, cut into fries
- Oil for frying
- 1 cup cheese curds
- 2 cups beef or mushroom gravy

**Instructions:**

1. Heat oil in a fryer to 375°F (190°C). Fry potatoes until golden. Drain on paper towels.
2. Place fries on a plate, top with cheese curds, and pour hot gravy over. Serve immediately.

# Roasted Root Vegetable Medley

**Ingredients:**

- 2 carrots, sliced
- 2 parsnips, sliced
- 1 sweet potato, cubed
- 1 tbsp olive oil
- 1 tsp dried rosemary
- Salt and pepper to taste

**Instructions:**

1. Preheat oven to 400°F (200°C).
2. Toss vegetables with oil, rosemary, salt, and pepper.
3. Roast for 35-40 minutes, stirring occasionally. Serve warm.

**Canadian Lentil Soup**

**Ingredients:**

- 1 cup lentils, rinsed
- 1 small onion, chopped
- 2 carrots, diced
- 3 cloves garlic, minced
- 4 cups vegetable broth
- 1 tsp cumin
- 1/2 tsp smoked paprika
- Salt and pepper to taste

**Instructions:**

1. Sauté onion, carrots, and garlic in a pot.
2. Add lentils, broth, and spices. Bring to a boil.
3. Simmer for 25-30 minutes until lentils are tender. Serve warm.

## Honey-Glazed Carrots and Parsnips

**Ingredients:**

- 2 carrots, sliced
- 2 parsnips, sliced
- 1 tbsp butter
- 1 tbsp honey
- 1/2 tsp salt

**Instructions:**

1. Sauté carrots and parsnips in butter for 5 minutes.
2. Drizzle with honey and salt. Cook until tender. Serve warm.

## Tourtière (French Canadian Meat Pie)

**Ingredients:**

- 1 lb ground pork
- 1/2 lb ground beef
- 1 small onion, finely chopped
- 2 cloves garlic, minced
- 1/2 tsp ground cinnamon
- 1/4 tsp ground cloves
- 1/2 tsp dried thyme
- 1/2 tsp salt
- 1/4 tsp black pepper
- 1/2 cup beef broth
- 1/2 cup mashed potatoes
- 1 double-crust pie dough

**Instructions:**

1. Preheat oven to 375°F (190°C).
2. In a pan, cook pork and beef over medium heat until browned. Drain excess fat.
3. Add onion, garlic, cinnamon, cloves, thyme, salt, and pepper. Cook until onions are soft.
4. Stir in broth and mashed potatoes. Let cool.
5. Roll out pie dough and place in a pie dish. Fill with meat mixture and cover with the second crust.
6. Crimp edges and cut slits in the top. Bake for 35-40 minutes until golden. Cool before serving.

**Maple Baked Beans**

**Ingredients:**

- 2 cups dried navy beans
- 4 cups water
- 1/2 cup pure maple syrup
- 1/2 cup ketchup
- 1 tbsp Dijon mustard
- 1 small onion, diced
- 4 slices bacon, chopped
- 1 tsp salt
- 1/2 tsp black pepper

**Instructions:**

1. Soak beans overnight. Drain and rinse.
2. In a pot, bring beans and water to a boil. Simmer for 1 hour.
3. Preheat oven to 300°F (150°C).
4. In a baking dish, mix beans with maple syrup, ketchup, mustard, onion, bacon, salt, and pepper.
5. Cover and bake for 3-4 hours, stirring occasionally. Serve warm.

## Apple and Cheddar Salad

**Ingredients:**

- 4 cups mixed greens
- 1 apple, thinly sliced
- 1/2 cup aged cheddar, cubed
- 1/4 cup toasted walnuts
- 2 tbsp dried cranberries
- 2 tbsp olive oil
- 1 tbsp apple cider vinegar
- 1 tsp honey
- Salt and pepper to taste

**Instructions:**

1. Arrange greens, apple slices, cheddar, walnuts, and cranberries in a bowl.
2. In a small bowl, whisk olive oil, vinegar, honey, salt, and pepper.
3. Drizzle dressing over salad and toss. Serve immediately.

## Wheat Berry and Cranberry Salad

**Ingredients:**

- 1 cup cooked wheat berries
- 1/2 cup dried cranberries
- 1/4 cup chopped pecans
- 1/4 cup diced celery
- 1/4 cup crumbled feta
- 2 tbsp olive oil
- 1 tbsp balsamic vinegar
- Salt and pepper to taste

**Instructions:**

1. In a bowl, combine wheat berries, cranberries, pecans, celery, and feta.
2. Whisk olive oil, vinegar, salt, and pepper.
3. Toss salad with dressing and serve.

## Elk and Mushroom Burgers

### Ingredients:

- 1 lb ground elk
- 1/2 cup mushrooms, finely chopped
- 1 small onion, minced
- 1 clove garlic, minced
- 1/2 tsp dried thyme
- 1/2 tsp salt
- 1/4 tsp black pepper
- 1 tbsp Worcestershire sauce
- 1 tbsp olive oil

### Instructions:

1. Mix all ingredients in a bowl.
2. Shape into patties and grill over medium heat for 4-5 minutes per side.
3. Serve on buns with preferred toppings.

# Chokecherry Syrup Pancakes

**Ingredients:**

**Pancakes:**

- 1 cup all-purpose flour
- 1 tbsp sugar
- 1 tsp baking powder
- 1/2 tsp baking soda
- 1/4 tsp salt
- 1 cup buttermilk
- 1 egg
- 1 tbsp melted butter

**Chokecherry Syrup:**

- 2 cups chokecherries
- 1 cup water
- 1 cup sugar

**Instructions:**

1. For syrup, simmer chokecherries and water for 15 minutes. Strain and return liquid to pot.
2. Add sugar and simmer until thickened.
3. For pancakes, mix dry ingredients. Whisk wet ingredients separately and combine.
4. Cook pancakes on a hot griddle until golden.
5. Serve with chokecherry syrup.

**Roasted Beets with Goat Cheese**

**Ingredients:**

- 3 beets, peeled and cubed
- 1 tbsp olive oil
- Salt and pepper to taste
- 1/4 cup crumbled goat cheese
- 1 tbsp balsamic glaze

**Instructions:**

1. Preheat oven to 400°F (200°C).
2. Toss beets with olive oil, salt, and pepper. Roast for 35-40 minutes.
3. Sprinkle with goat cheese and drizzle with balsamic glaze. Serve warm.

## Smoked Trout with Horseradish Cream

**Ingredients:**

- 2 smoked trout fillets
- 1/2 cup sour cream
- 1 tbsp prepared horseradish
- 1 tbsp lemon juice
- 1 tbsp chopped dill
- Salt and pepper to taste

**Instructions:**

1. In a bowl, mix sour cream, horseradish, lemon juice, dill, salt, and pepper.
2. Serve smoked trout with horseradish cream on the side.

## Barley and Vegetable Stuffed Peppers

**Ingredients:**

- 4 bell peppers, halved and seeded
- 1 cup cooked barley
- 1 small zucchini, diced
- 1 small carrot, grated
- 1/2 cup diced tomatoes
- 1/2 tsp dried oregano
- Salt and pepper to taste
- 1/2 cup shredded cheese

**Instructions:**

1. Preheat oven to 375°F (190°C).
2. In a bowl, mix barley, zucchini, carrot, tomatoes, oregano, salt, and pepper.
3. Fill peppers with mixture and top with cheese.
4. Bake for 25-30 minutes. Serve warm.

## Split Pea and Ham Soup

**Ingredients:**

- 1 cup dried split peas, rinsed
- 1 small onion, chopped
- 1 carrot, diced
- 2 cloves garlic, minced
- 4 cups chicken broth
- 1 cup diced ham
- 1 bay leaf
- 1/2 tsp dried thyme
- Salt and pepper to taste

**Instructions:**

1. In a pot, sauté onion, carrot, and garlic.
2. Add peas, broth, ham, bay leaf, thyme, salt, and pepper.
3. Bring to a boil, then simmer for 45-50 minutes until peas are soft.
4. Remove bay leaf and serve warm.

## Sweet Corn Fritters

**Ingredients:**

- 1 cup fresh or frozen corn kernels
- 1/2 cup all-purpose flour
- 1/4 cup cornmeal
- 1/2 tsp baking powder
- 1/2 tsp salt
- 1/4 tsp black pepper
- 1/4 cup milk
- 1 egg
- 1 tbsp chopped green onions
- 1 tbsp butter or oil for frying

**Instructions:**

1. In a bowl, mix flour, cornmeal, baking powder, salt, and pepper.
2. Stir in milk, egg, and green onions. Fold in corn.
3. Heat butter in a skillet over medium heat. Drop spoonfuls of batter and cook for 2-3 minutes per side until golden.
4. Serve warm.

## Maple-Glazed Salmon

**Ingredients:**

- 2 salmon fillets
- 1/4 cup pure maple syrup
- 1 tbsp Dijon mustard
- 1 tbsp soy sauce
- 1 tsp lemon juice
- 1/2 tsp black pepper

**Instructions:**

1. Preheat oven to 400°F (200°C).
2. In a small bowl, mix maple syrup, mustard, soy sauce, lemon juice, and pepper.
3. Place salmon on a baking sheet and brush with glaze.
4. Bake for 12-15 minutes until flaky. Serve warm.

## Rye Bread with Flax Seeds

**Ingredients:**

- 2 cups rye flour
- 1 cup all-purpose flour
- 1/4 cup ground flax seeds
- 1 packet (2 1/4 tsp) active dry yeast
- 1 tsp salt
- 1 cup warm water
- 1 tbsp honey
- 1 tbsp olive oil

**Instructions:**

1. Dissolve yeast in warm water with honey. Let sit for 5 minutes.
2. In a bowl, mix flours, flax seeds, and salt. Add yeast mixture and olive oil.
3. Knead for 8-10 minutes until smooth. Cover and let rise for 1 hour.
4. Shape into a loaf, place in a greased pan, and let rise for another 30 minutes.
5. Preheat oven to 375°F (190°C) and bake for 30-35 minutes. Cool before slicing.

**Grilled Asparagus with Lemon Butter**

**Ingredients:**

- 1 bunch asparagus, trimmed
- 1 tbsp olive oil
- 2 tbsp butter, melted
- 1 tsp lemon zest
- 1 tbsp lemon juice
- Salt and pepper to taste

**Instructions:**

1. Preheat grill to medium heat. Toss asparagus with olive oil, salt, and pepper.
2. Grill for 4-5 minutes, turning occasionally.
3. Mix melted butter with lemon zest and juice. Drizzle over asparagus before serving.

**Baked Oatmeal with Blueberries**

**Ingredients:**

- 2 cups rolled oats
- 1/4 cup maple syrup
- 1 tsp baking powder
- 1/2 tsp cinnamon
- 1/4 tsp salt
- 1 1/2 cups milk
- 1 egg
- 1 tsp vanilla extract
- 1 cup fresh or frozen blueberries

**Instructions:**

1. Preheat oven to 350°F (175°C).
2. In a bowl, mix oats, baking powder, cinnamon, and salt.
3. In another bowl, whisk milk, egg, vanilla, and maple syrup. Combine with dry ingredients.
4. Fold in blueberries and pour into a greased baking dish.
5. Bake for 30-35 minutes until golden. Serve warm.

**Wild Blueberry Scones**

**Ingredients:**

- 2 cups all-purpose flour
- 1/4 cup sugar
- 1 tbsp baking powder
- 1/2 tsp salt
- 1/2 cup butter, cold and cubed
- 1/2 cup milk
- 1 egg
- 1 tsp vanilla extract
- 1 cup wild blueberries

**Instructions:**

1. Preheat oven to 375°F (190°C).
2. In a bowl, mix flour, sugar, baking powder, and salt.
3. Cut in butter until mixture is crumbly.
4. Whisk milk, egg, and vanilla, then add to dry ingredients.
5. Fold in blueberries. Shape dough into a disc and cut into wedges.
6. Bake for 18-20 minutes until golden.

## Beef and Barley Hotpot

**Ingredients:**

- 1 lb beef stew meat, cubed
- 1 tbsp oil
- 1 onion, chopped
- 2 carrots, diced
- 2 celery stalks, chopped
- 3 cloves garlic, minced
- 1/2 cup pearl barley
- 4 cups beef broth
- 1 tsp dried thyme
- 1 bay leaf
- Salt and pepper to taste

**Instructions:**

1. Heat oil in a pot and brown beef. Remove and set aside.
2. Sauté onion, carrots, celery, and garlic until soft.
3. Add barley, beef, broth, thyme, bay leaf, salt, and pepper.
4. Simmer for 1.5 hours until beef is tender. Remove bay leaf before serving.

## Roasted Pumpkin Soup

**Ingredients:**

- 4 cups pumpkin, cubed
- 1 small onion, chopped
- 2 cloves garlic, minced
- 3 cups vegetable broth
- 1/2 cup coconut milk
- 1 tsp ground cumin
- 1/2 tsp cinnamon
- Salt and pepper to taste
- 1 tbsp olive oil

**Instructions:**

1. Preheat oven to 400°F (200°C). Toss pumpkin with olive oil and roast for 25-30 minutes.
2. In a pot, sauté onion and garlic until soft. Add roasted pumpkin.
3. Pour in broth and bring to a simmer. Blend until smooth.
4. Stir in coconut milk, cumin, cinnamon, salt, and pepper. Simmer for 5 more minutes. Serve warm.

## Cranberry-Maple Turkey Meatballs

**Ingredients:**

- 1 lb ground turkey
- 1/4 cup breadcrumbs
- 1/4 cup dried cranberries, chopped
- 1 egg
- 1 tbsp maple syrup
- 1/2 tsp dried sage
- 1/2 tsp salt
- 1/4 tsp black pepper
- 1 tbsp olive oil

**Instructions:**

1. Preheat oven to 375°F (190°C).
2. In a bowl, mix turkey, breadcrumbs, cranberries, egg, maple syrup, sage, salt, and pepper.
3. Shape into small meatballs.
4. Heat olive oil in a skillet and brown meatballs on all sides.
5. Transfer to a baking dish and bake for 15 minutes until cooked through. Serve warm.

## Homemade Saskatoon Berry Jam

**Ingredients:**

- 4 cups Saskatoon berries
- 1 1/2 cups sugar
- 1/4 cup lemon juice
- 1/2 cup water
- 1 packet (1.75 oz) pectin

**Instructions:**

1. In a pot, combine berries, sugar, lemon juice, and water. Simmer for 10 minutes.
2. Mash berries slightly and stir in pectin. Bring to a rolling boil for 1 minute.
3. Pour into sterilized jars and seal. Let cool before storing.

**Creamy Potato and Leek Soup**

**Ingredients:**

- 3 large potatoes, peeled and diced
- 2 leeks, chopped
- 3 cups vegetable broth
- 1/2 cup heavy cream
- 2 tbsp butter
- 2 cloves garlic, minced
- Salt and pepper to taste

**Instructions:**

1. In a pot, melt butter and sauté leeks and garlic until soft.
2. Add potatoes and broth. Simmer for 20 minutes.
3. Blend until smooth, then stir in cream. Season to taste and serve warm.

## Barley Risotto with Mushrooms

**Ingredients:**

- 1 cup pearl barley
- 3 cups vegetable broth
- 1 cup mushrooms, sliced
- 1 small onion, diced
- 2 cloves garlic, minced
- 1/4 cup grated Parmesan
- 1 tbsp butter
- Salt and pepper to taste

**Instructions:**

1. Sauté onion, garlic, and mushrooms in butter until soft.
2. Add barley and cook for 2 minutes.
3. Gradually add broth, stirring frequently, until barley is tender.
4. Stir in Parmesan, salt, and pepper before serving.

## Maple-Dijon Glazed Pork Chops

**Ingredients:**

- 2 pork chops
- 1/4 cup pure maple syrup
- 1 tbsp Dijon mustard
- 1 tbsp soy sauce
- 1/2 tsp black pepper

**Instructions:**

1. Preheat oven to 375°F (190°C).
2. Mix maple syrup, mustard, soy sauce, and pepper.
3. Brush glaze on pork chops and bake for 20-25 minutes, basting halfway through.
4. Serve warm.

## Oatmeal Maple Cookies

**Ingredients:**

- 1 cup rolled oats
- 1 cup all-purpose flour
- 1/2 cup butter, softened
- 1/2 cup maple syrup
- 1/2 tsp cinnamon
- 1/2 tsp baking soda
- 1/4 tsp salt
- 1 egg

**Instructions:**

1. Preheat oven to 350°F (175°C).
2. In a bowl, mix oats, flour, cinnamon, baking soda, and salt.
3. In another bowl, cream butter and maple syrup. Beat in egg.
4. Combine wet and dry ingredients.
5. Drop spoonfuls onto a baking sheet and bake for 10-12 minutes.

## Sunflower Seed Granola

**Ingredients:**

- 2 cups rolled oats
- 1/2 cup sunflower seeds
- 1/4 cup honey
- 1/4 cup maple syrup
- 2 tbsp coconut oil
- 1/2 tsp cinnamon

**Instructions:**

1. Preheat oven to 325°F (165°C).
2. Mix oats, sunflower seeds, and cinnamon in a bowl.
3. In a saucepan, heat honey, maple syrup, and coconut oil until combined.
4. Pour over oat mixture and toss. Spread on a baking sheet.
5. Bake for 20 minutes, stirring halfway. Cool before serving.

## Canadian Cheddar Biscuits

**Ingredients:**

- 2 cups all-purpose flour
- 1 tbsp baking powder
- 1/2 tsp salt
- 1/2 cup cold butter, cubed
- 1 cup grated Canadian cheddar
- 3/4 cup milk

**Instructions:**

1. Preheat oven to 375°F (190°C).
2. Mix flour, baking powder, and salt in a bowl.
3. Cut in butter until mixture is crumbly. Stir in cheddar.
4. Add milk and mix until dough forms.
5. Drop spoonfuls onto a baking sheet and bake for 15-18 minutes.

**Honey-Garlic Glazed Chicken Thighs**

**Ingredients:**

- 4 bone-in chicken thighs
- 1/4 cup honey
- 2 tbsp soy sauce
- 2 cloves garlic, minced
- 1 tbsp olive oil
- 1/2 tsp black pepper

**Instructions:**

1. Preheat oven to 375°F (190°C).
2. Mix honey, soy sauce, garlic, olive oil, and pepper.
3. Place chicken in a baking dish and brush with glaze.
4. Bake for 35-40 minutes, basting occasionally. Serve warm.

# Roasted Garlic and Butternut Squash Soup

**Ingredients:**

- 1 butternut squash, peeled and cubed
- 1 head garlic, roasted
- 1 small onion, diced
- 3 cups vegetable broth
- 1/2 cup coconut milk
- 1 tbsp olive oil
- 1/2 tsp ground nutmeg
- Salt and pepper to taste

**Instructions:**

1. Preheat oven to 400°F (200°C). Toss squash with olive oil and roast for 30 minutes.
2. In a pot, sauté onion until soft. Squeeze in roasted garlic.
3. Add squash and broth. Simmer for 10 minutes.
4. Blend until smooth, stir in coconut milk, nutmeg, salt, and pepper. Serve warm.

# Bison Meatloaf with Wild Rice

**Ingredients:**

- 1 lb ground bison
- 1/2 cup cooked wild rice
- 1 small onion, chopped
- 1 egg
- 1/4 cup breadcrumbs
- 2 tbsp ketchup
- 1 tbsp Worcestershire sauce
- 1/2 tsp salt
- 1/4 tsp black pepper

**Instructions:**

1. Preheat oven to 375°F (190°C).
2. In a bowl, mix all ingredients until well combined.
3. Shape into a loaf and place in a greased pan.
4. Bake for 45-50 minutes until cooked through. Let rest before slicing.

## Carrot and Apple Slaw

**Ingredients:**

- 2 cups shredded carrots
- 1 apple, julienned
- 1/4 cup raisins
- 1/4 cup chopped walnuts
- 2 tbsp apple cider vinegar
- 1 tbsp honey
- 1 tbsp olive oil
- 1/2 tsp salt
- 1/4 tsp black pepper

**Instructions:**

1. In a large bowl, combine carrots, apple, raisins, and walnuts.
2. In a small bowl, whisk together apple cider vinegar, honey, olive oil, salt, and pepper.
3. Pour dressing over the slaw and toss to coat.
4. Let sit for 15 minutes before serving.

## Roasted Brussels Sprouts with Maple Bacon

**Ingredients:**

- 1 lb Brussels sprouts, halved
- 4 slices bacon, chopped
- 2 tbsp pure maple syrup
- 1 tbsp olive oil
- 1/2 tsp salt
- 1/4 tsp black pepper

**Instructions:**

1. Preheat oven to 400°F (200°C).
2. Toss Brussels sprouts with olive oil, salt, and pepper.
3. Spread on a baking sheet and sprinkle with bacon.
4. Roast for 20-25 minutes, stirring occasionally.
5. Drizzle with maple syrup and roast for 5 more minutes. Serve warm.

## Barbecue Bison Ribs

**Ingredients:**

- 2 lbs bison ribs
- 1 cup barbecue sauce
- 1/4 cup apple cider vinegar
- 2 cloves garlic, minced
- 1 tbsp smoked paprika
- 1 tsp salt
- 1/2 tsp black pepper

**Instructions:**

1. Preheat oven to 300°F (150°C).
2. Season ribs with paprika, salt, and pepper.
3. Wrap in foil and bake for 2.5-3 hours until tender.
4. In a saucepan, mix barbecue sauce, vinegar, and garlic. Simmer for 10 minutes.
5. Brush ribs with sauce and grill over medium heat for 5 minutes per side.
6. Serve with extra sauce.

**Farmer's Market Vegetable Stir-Fry**

**Ingredients:**

- 1 small zucchini, sliced
- 1 red bell pepper, sliced
- 1 cup snap peas
- 1 small carrot, julienned
- 2 cloves garlic, minced
- 1 tbsp soy sauce
- 1 tbsp sesame oil
- 1/2 tsp ginger, grated
- 1 tbsp sesame seeds

**Instructions:**

1. Heat sesame oil in a pan over medium-high heat.
2. Add garlic and ginger, sauté for 30 seconds.
3. Stir in vegetables and cook for 4-5 minutes until tender-crisp.
4. Add soy sauce and toss to coat.
5. Sprinkle with sesame seeds before serving.

## Creamy Corn Chowder

**Ingredients:**

- 2 tbsp butter
- 1 small onion, diced
- 2 cloves garlic, minced
- 2 medium potatoes, diced
- 3 cups corn kernels (fresh or frozen)
- 3 cups vegetable or chicken broth
- 1 cup heavy cream
- 1/2 tsp dried thyme
- Salt and pepper to taste
- 2 tbsp chopped fresh parsley

**Instructions:**

1. In a pot, melt butter over medium heat. Sauté onion and garlic until soft.
2. Add potatoes, corn, broth, thyme, salt, and pepper. Simmer for 15 minutes until potatoes are tender.
3. Stir in heavy cream and cook for 5 more minutes.
4. Garnish with parsley and serve warm.

## Rhubarb Crisp with Oat Topping

**Ingredients:**

**Filling:**

- 4 cups rhubarb, chopped
- 1/2 cup sugar
- 1 tbsp cornstarch
- 1 tsp vanilla extract

**Topping:**

- 1 cup rolled oats
- 1/2 cup all-purpose flour
- 1/3 cup brown sugar
- 1/2 tsp cinnamon
- 1/2 cup butter, melted

**Instructions:**

1. Preheat oven to 375°F (190°C).
2. Toss rhubarb with sugar, cornstarch, and vanilla. Spread in a baking dish.
3. Mix oats, flour, brown sugar, cinnamon, and melted butter. Sprinkle over rhubarb.
4. Bake for 35-40 minutes until golden and bubbly. Serve warm.

## Maple Butter Tarts

**Ingredients:**

**Pastry:**

- 1 1/4 cups all-purpose flour
- 1/2 cup cold butter, cubed
- 1/4 tsp salt
- 3 tbsp cold water

**Filling:**

- 1/2 cup brown sugar
- 1/2 cup pure maple syrup
- 1/4 cup melted butter
- 1 egg, beaten
- 1 tsp vanilla extract
- 1/2 cup raisins or chopped pecans

**Instructions:**

1. Preheat oven to 375°F (190°C).
2. For pastry, mix flour and salt. Cut in butter until crumbly. Add water and mix until dough forms. Chill for 30 minutes.
3. Roll out dough and cut into rounds. Place in tart tins.
4. Whisk filling ingredients and pour into shells.
5. Bake for 20-25 minutes until filling is set. Cool before serving.

**Venison Sausage with Roasted Apples**

**Ingredients:**

- 4 venison sausages
- 2 apples, sliced
- 1 tbsp olive oil
- 1 tbsp maple syrup
- 1/2 tsp cinnamon
- Salt and pepper to taste

**Instructions:**

1. Preheat oven to 375°F (190°C).
2. Toss apple slices with olive oil, maple syrup, cinnamon, salt, and pepper.
3. Spread apples on a baking sheet and place sausages on top.
4. Roast for 25-30 minutes, turning sausages halfway. Serve warm.

# Spelt Flour Pancakes with Berries

**Ingredients:**

- 1 cup spelt flour
- 1 tsp baking powder
- 1/4 tsp salt
- 1 tbsp maple syrup
- 1 egg
- 3/4 cup milk
- 1/2 tsp vanilla extract
- 1 tbsp melted butter
- 1/2 cup fresh or frozen berries

**Instructions:**

1. In a bowl, mix spelt flour, baking powder, and salt.
2. Whisk in maple syrup, egg, milk, vanilla, and melted butter.
3. Heat a skillet and pour batter in small rounds. Cook until bubbles form, then flip.
4. Serve with berries and extra maple syrup.

# Roasted Chestnut and Mushroom Soup

**Ingredients:**

- 1 cup roasted chestnuts, chopped
- 1 cup mushrooms, sliced
- 1 small onion, chopped
- 2 cloves garlic, minced
- 3 cups vegetable broth
- 1/2 cup heavy cream
- 1 tbsp olive oil
- 1/2 tsp thyme
- Salt and pepper to taste

**Instructions:**

1. In a pot, heat olive oil and sauté onion, garlic, and mushrooms until soft.
2. Add chestnuts, broth, thyme, salt, and pepper. Simmer for 15 minutes.
3. Blend until smooth, then stir in heavy cream. Serve warm.

**Pumpkin Seed and Cranberry Energy Bites**

**Ingredients:**

- 1 cup rolled oats
- 1/2 cup pumpkin seeds
- 1/4 cup dried cranberries
- 1/4 cup honey
- 1/4 cup almond butter
- 1/2 tsp cinnamon

**Instructions:**

1. In a bowl, mix oats, pumpkin seeds, cranberries, cinnamon, honey, and almond butter.
2. Roll into small balls and refrigerate for 30 minutes before serving.

www.ingramcontent.com/pod-product-compliance
Lightning Source LLC
LaVergne TN
LVHW081332060526
838201LV00055B/2604

*9798348561420*